AF256138

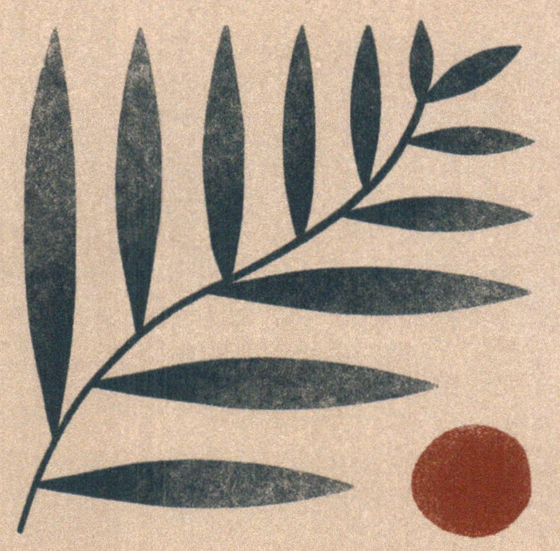

The Etymology
of
You and Me

By Jessica Covella
illustrated by Mariia Pleshakova

An Anthology of Poems about Words, Love,
and The Phases of The Moon

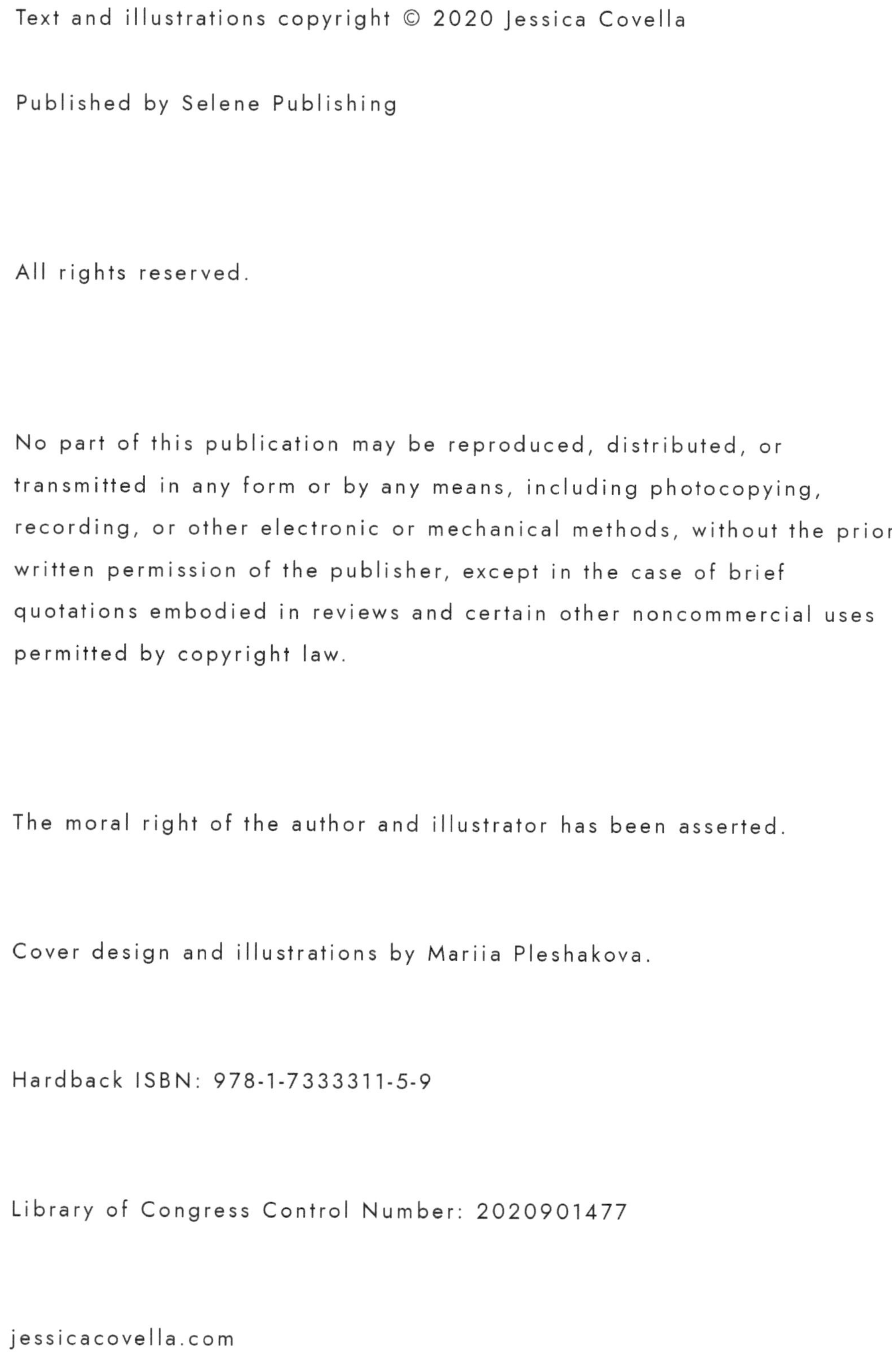

Published by Selene Publishing

Cover design and illustrations by Mariia Pleshakova.

Hardback ISBN: 978-1-7333311-5-9

Library of Congress Control Number: 2020901477

jessicacovella.com

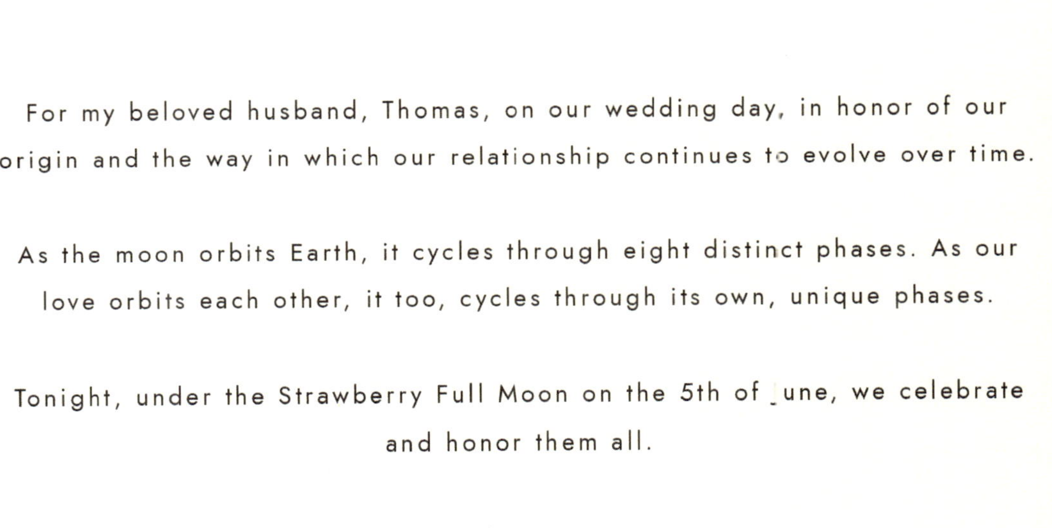

For my beloved husband, Thomas, on our wedding day, in honor of our origin and the way in which our relationship continues to evolve over time.

As the moon orbits Earth, it cycles through eight distinct phases. As our love orbits each other, it too, cycles through its own, unique phases.

Tonight, under the Strawberry Full Moon on the 5th of June, we celebrate and honor them all.

Love,

Jessica

et·y·mol·o·gy

/ˌedəˈmäləjē/

noun

1. the study of the origin of words and the way in which their meanings
have changed throughout history.

Origin

late Middle English: from Old French ethimologie, via Latin from Greek
etumologia, from etumologos 'student of etymology', from etumon,
neuter singular of etumos 'true'
("Etymology," 2020).

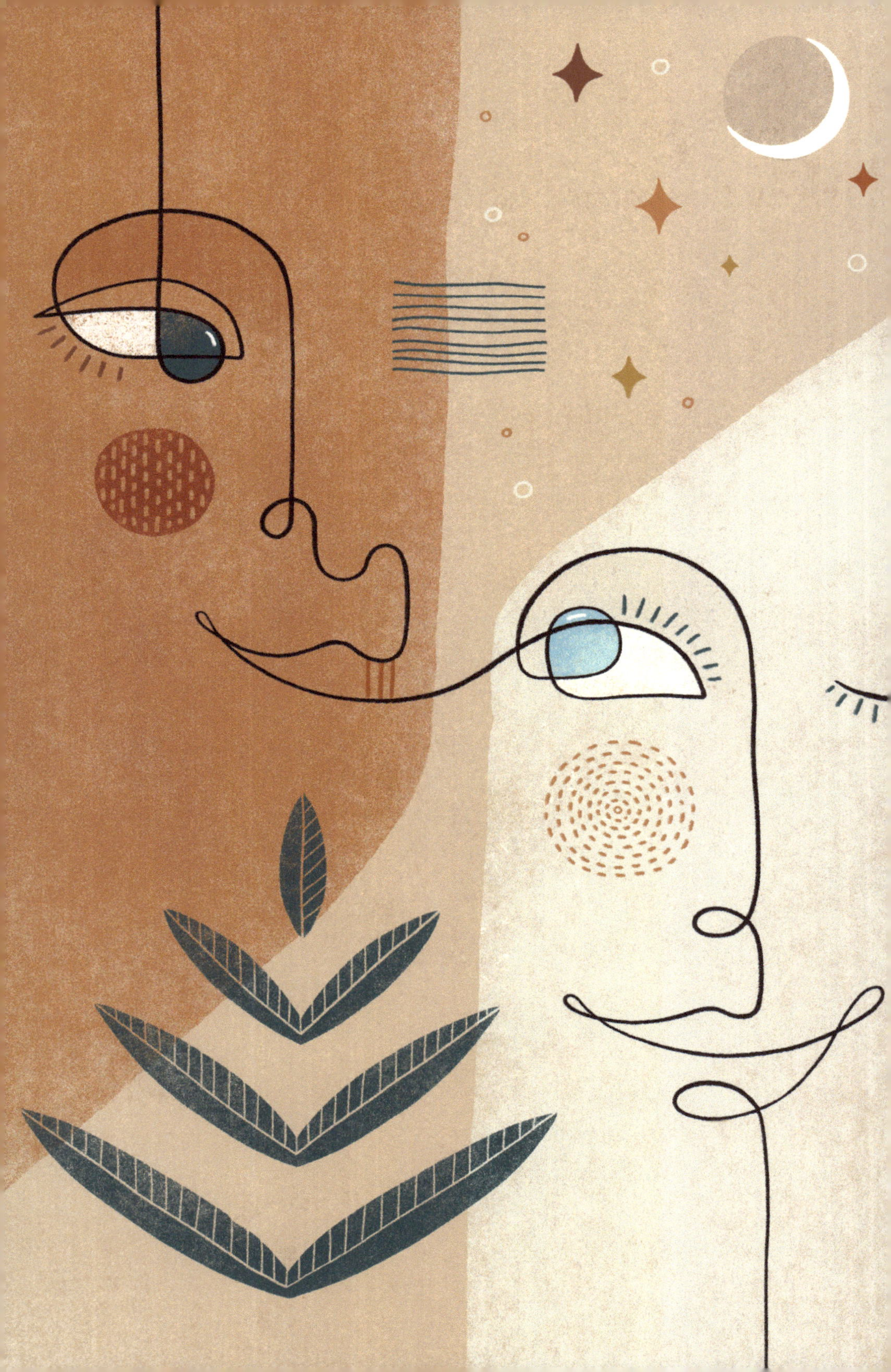

1

frolic

Joy

Laughter

B

U

B

B

L

E

S

of

s i l l i n e s s

Floating into the ether surrounded by our *smiles*.

Comfort like i have never known.

Our arms around one another,

ROMPING, ROLLING,

throwing pillows and jokes and kisses . . .

Creases of contentment appear around your eyes

and the corners of your mouth

as we enjoy a shared *CACHINNATION*!

so

deep

that my cells, mind, heart, and soul rejuvenate and *REJOICE!*

at how much c o l o r you have brought into my life.

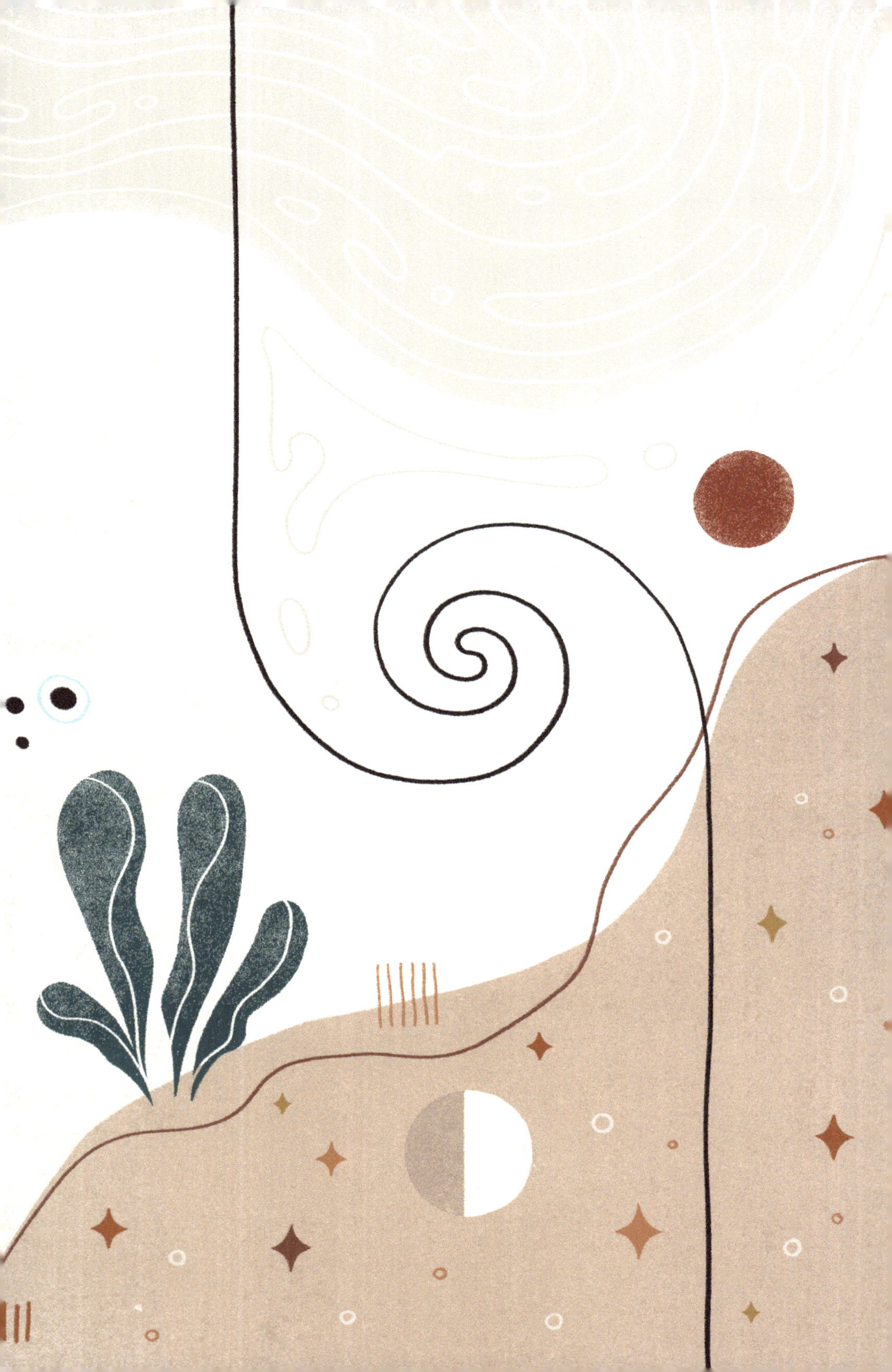

explosive expansion

No one tells you that when you

fall

in

love

all AXIOMS, especially ones of a mathematical nature,
become challenged by something so splendidly spiritual

that you begin to believe in an entirely

new layer

of presence & world

Actuality becomes e

f

f

e

r

v

e

s

c

e

n

t

and you experience a profound

joy in

p e r m e a t i n g the previously defined bounds
of what you knew and understood to be

possible

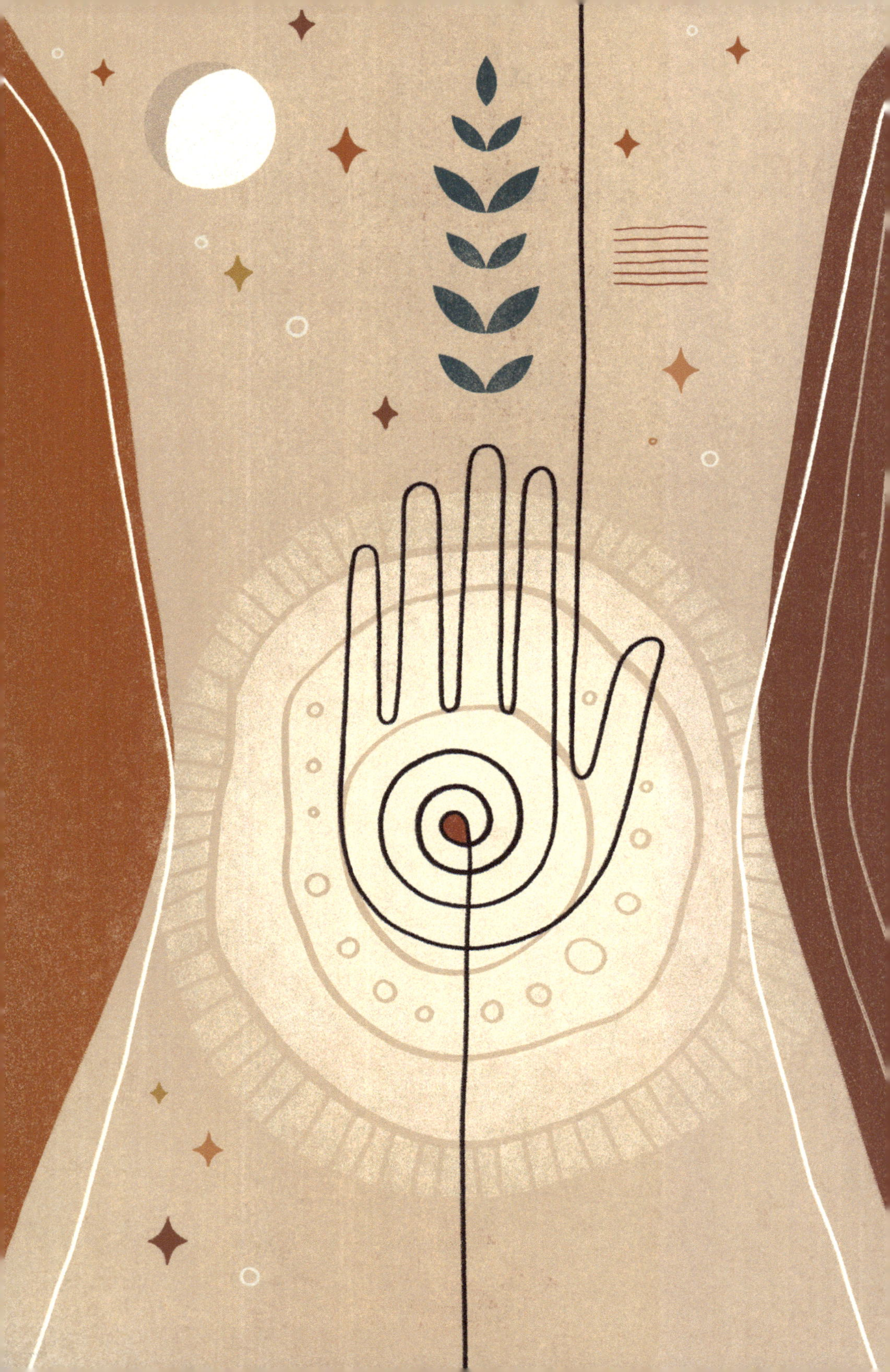

3

another world

How is it that you touch

me

so, so, so

that i leave this world and e n t e r

another?

Of ecstasy and spirit

Of ebullience and embrace

<pre>
            C   C
         O   A
of   N   &   R
      T   E
         A   S
           C   S
              T
</pre>

brushing, converging, merging and massaging

your hands up and down my body

up and down my body

up

and down

my body

Until, *standing outside of myself,*

all i see

is

l i g h t

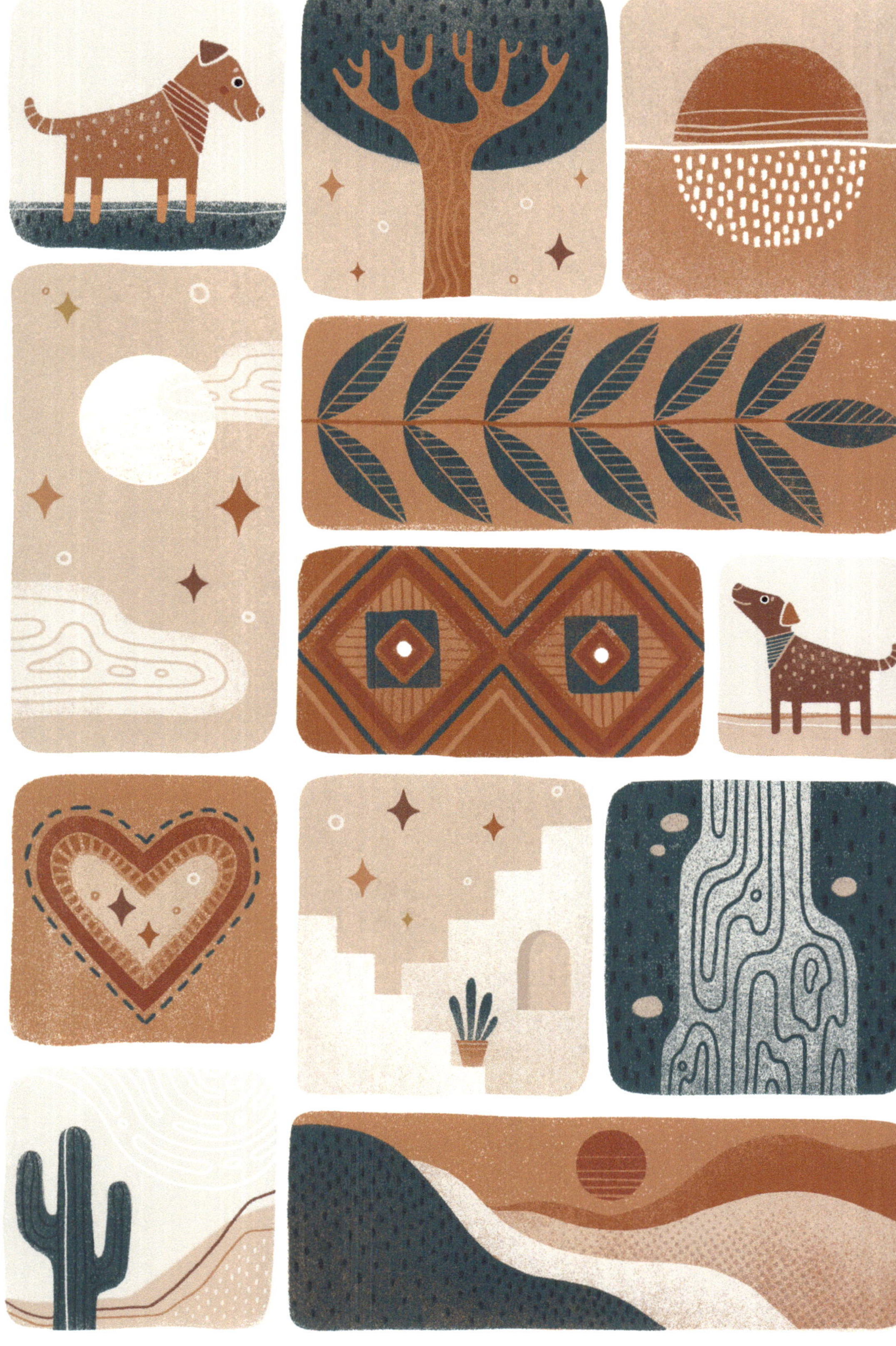

bricolage

Your father's pointedness,

and his heart

that time we walked under holiday lights aglow and ate shrimp
cocktail while sipping on champagne on an outdoor patio all to
ourselves in late November

when you danced around our kitchen, *skipping, laughing,*
until i *laughed* too!

my education, my travels, how i became a new level of wisdom
living in argentina, living in spain, learning to understand
the glory and the pain of being alone
in the presence of
myself

¡Mi español!
La expresión de mi entero, por las partes
matizadas de los dos idiomas, de ser
bilingüe

your mind and my mind
together

north carolina and
colorado

your memories and my memories
together

o u r m e m o r i e s

how you love seafood & data
truth & knowledge

two puppies, books,
when you proposed on the highway
when i proposed on your parents' couch

the full moon

the time we got married, and created the most beautiful

b r i   l a g e
c o   i have ever seen.

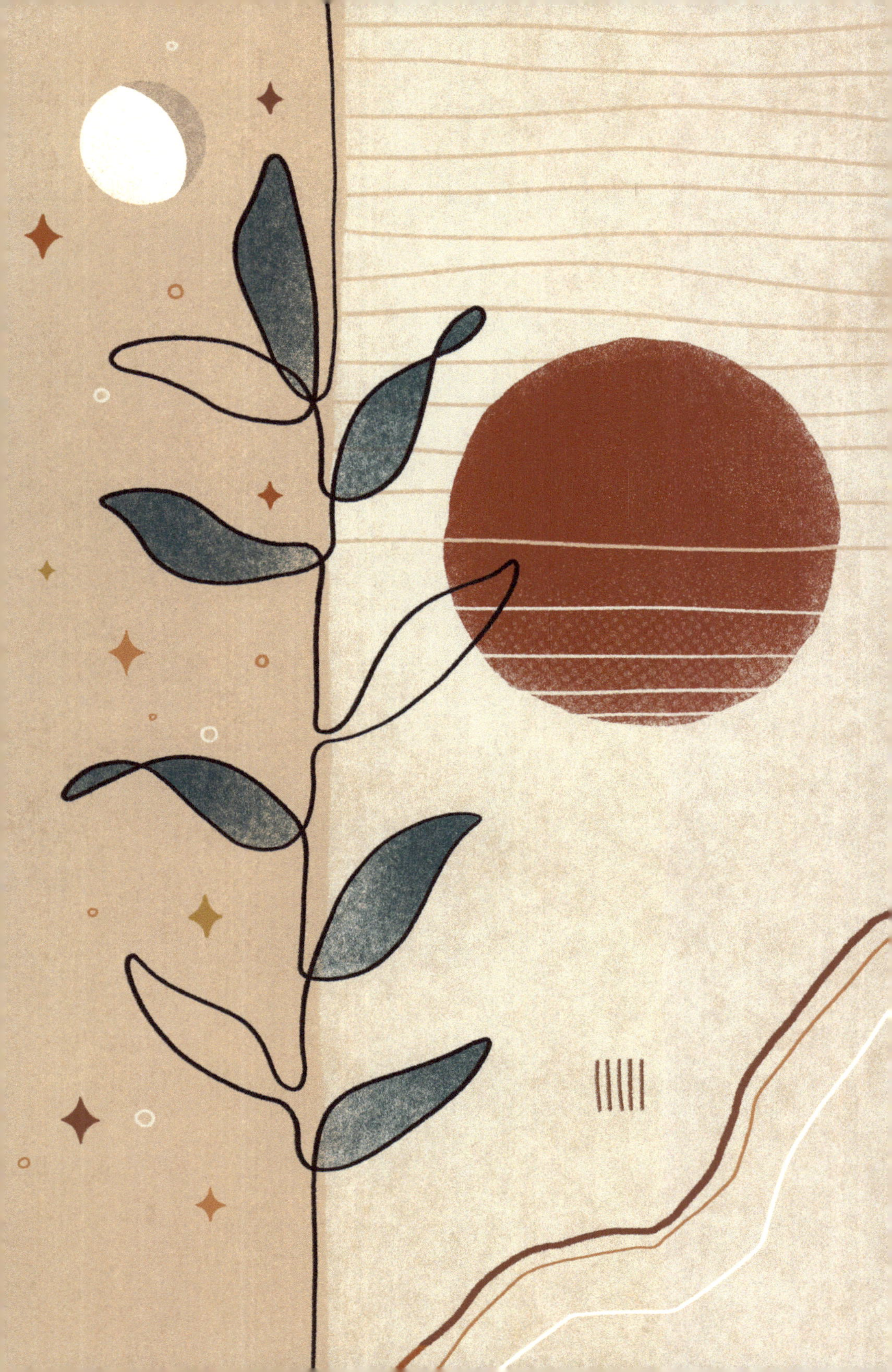

vicissitudes of love

Natural and welcomed are the vicissitudes of our

Love,

the **contrast** between the you and the me

A cacophony of celebrating the individuality of each of our souls,

our beings

Becoming the us

when you look *closely*,

there is more s i m i l a r i t y than d i f f e r e n c e

between each phase, each turn of season,

as you realize that which exists in them all:

PURPOSE (itself)

and

A DEEPER UNDERSTANDING

of the cycles (themselves)

and their consubstantial teachings

about life and change, growth and meaning,

cognition and insight,

and,

the *ups* and *downs* and *all arounds*

of

love.

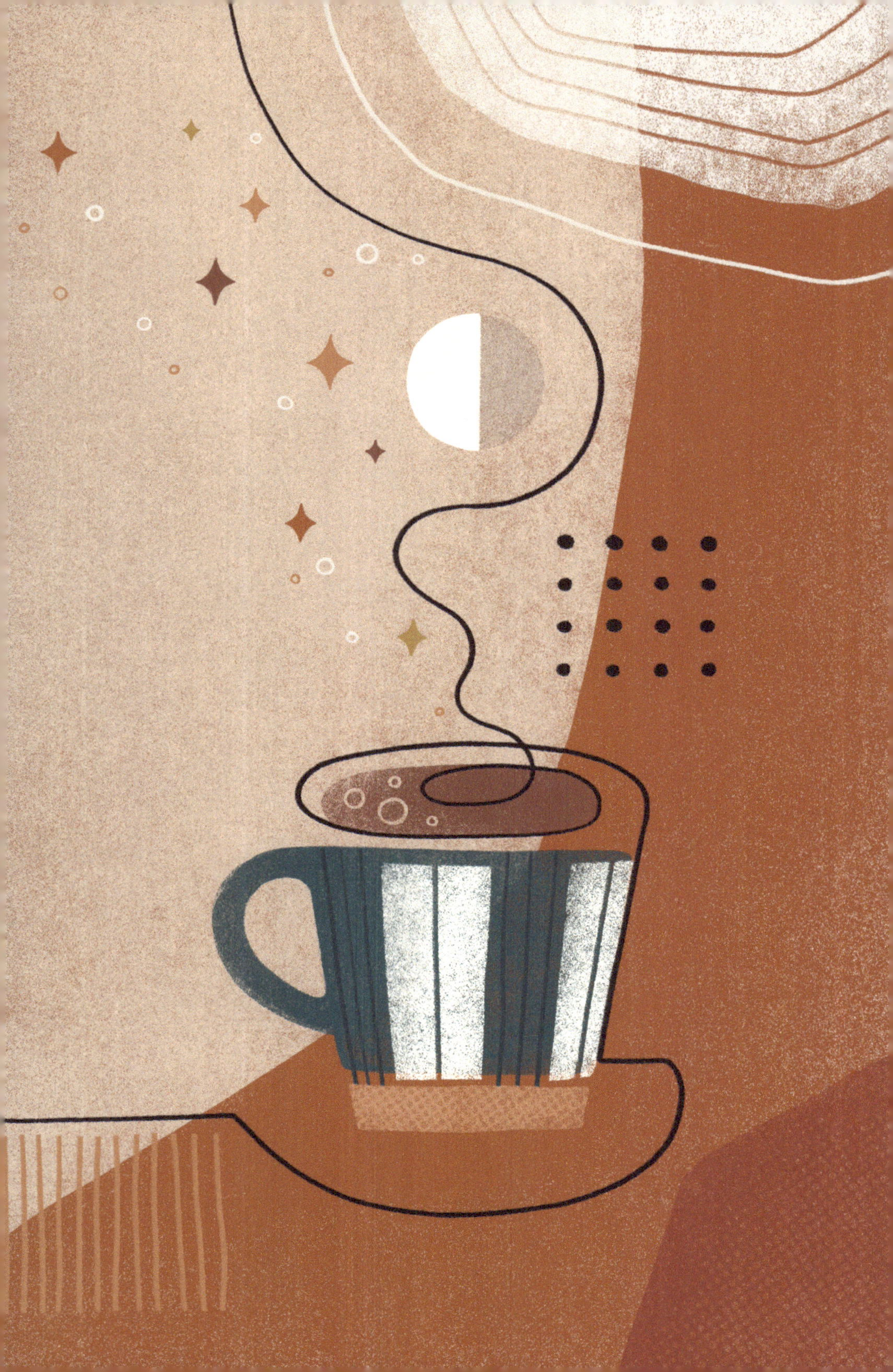

i can tell that we are going to be friends

You take the dogs out, early morning, so i can sleep

so i can "slumber" as you call it,

resetting, relaxing, coming back into myself.

You set a mug of coffee on my nightstand,

to be there when i wake

The *forethought* i feel for your wellbeing

And all that you are! And all that you want to be!

breathes through me.

You offer me space and forgiveness,

as only a true friend knows how to do

You offer me closeness and comradery,

as only a true friend knows how to do

You hold me accountable to being in

alignment with myself,

as only a true friend knows how to do

Even in our s e p a r a t e n e s s

We are *together*

Have i ever told you that our *consonance*

is my most venerated component of our relationship?

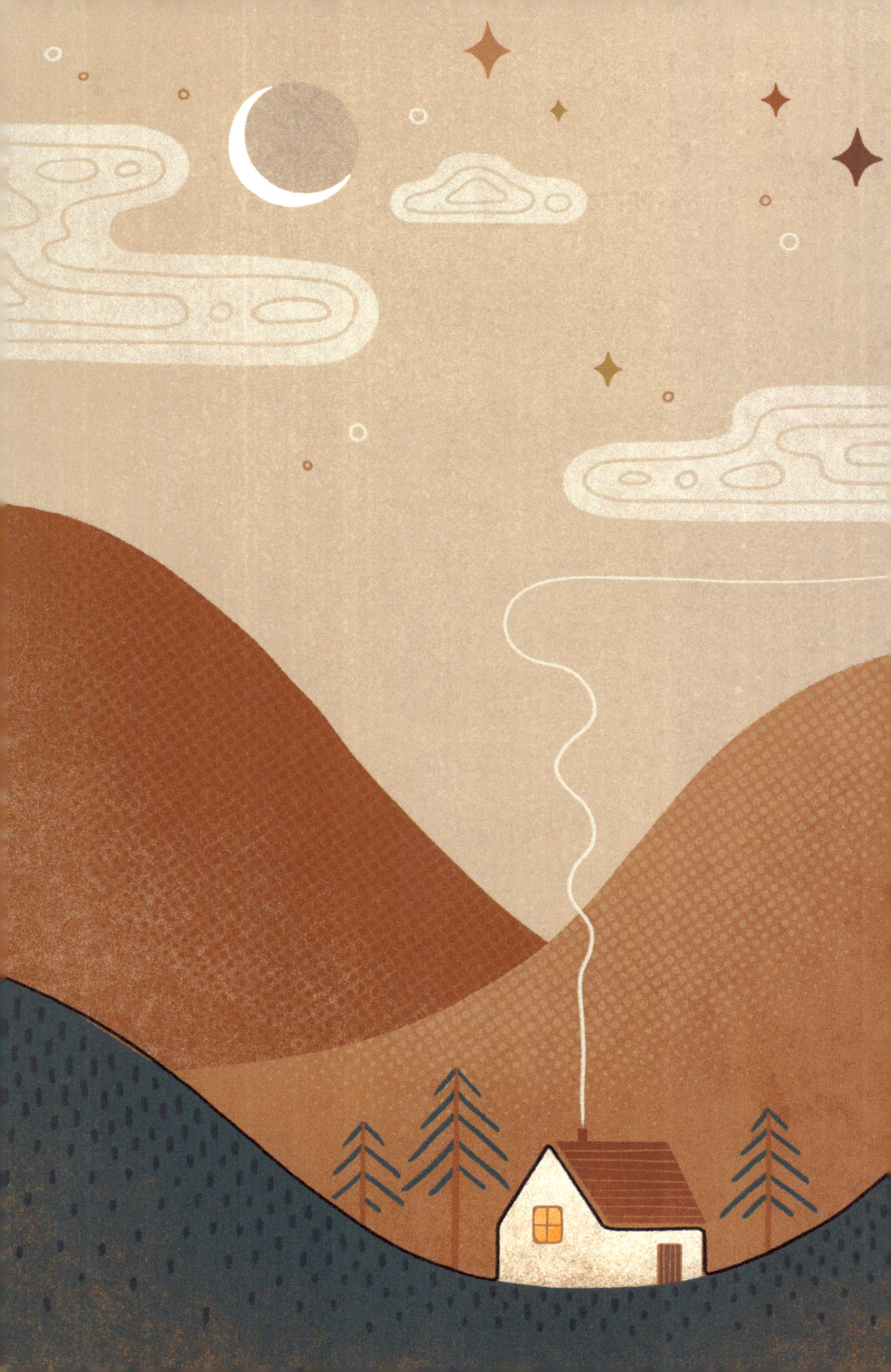

home

i find home

in a part of you.

seeing you, seeing me

feeling you, feeling me

moving from a place

to a state

to a formative belief

of being found,

of being

h o m e.

you have somehow been there all along,

for each of the triumphs

and the defeats

because when i met you and you took my hand,

bearing witness to the truth of who i am

you said

yes

and i said

yes

this is where

we are meant to be

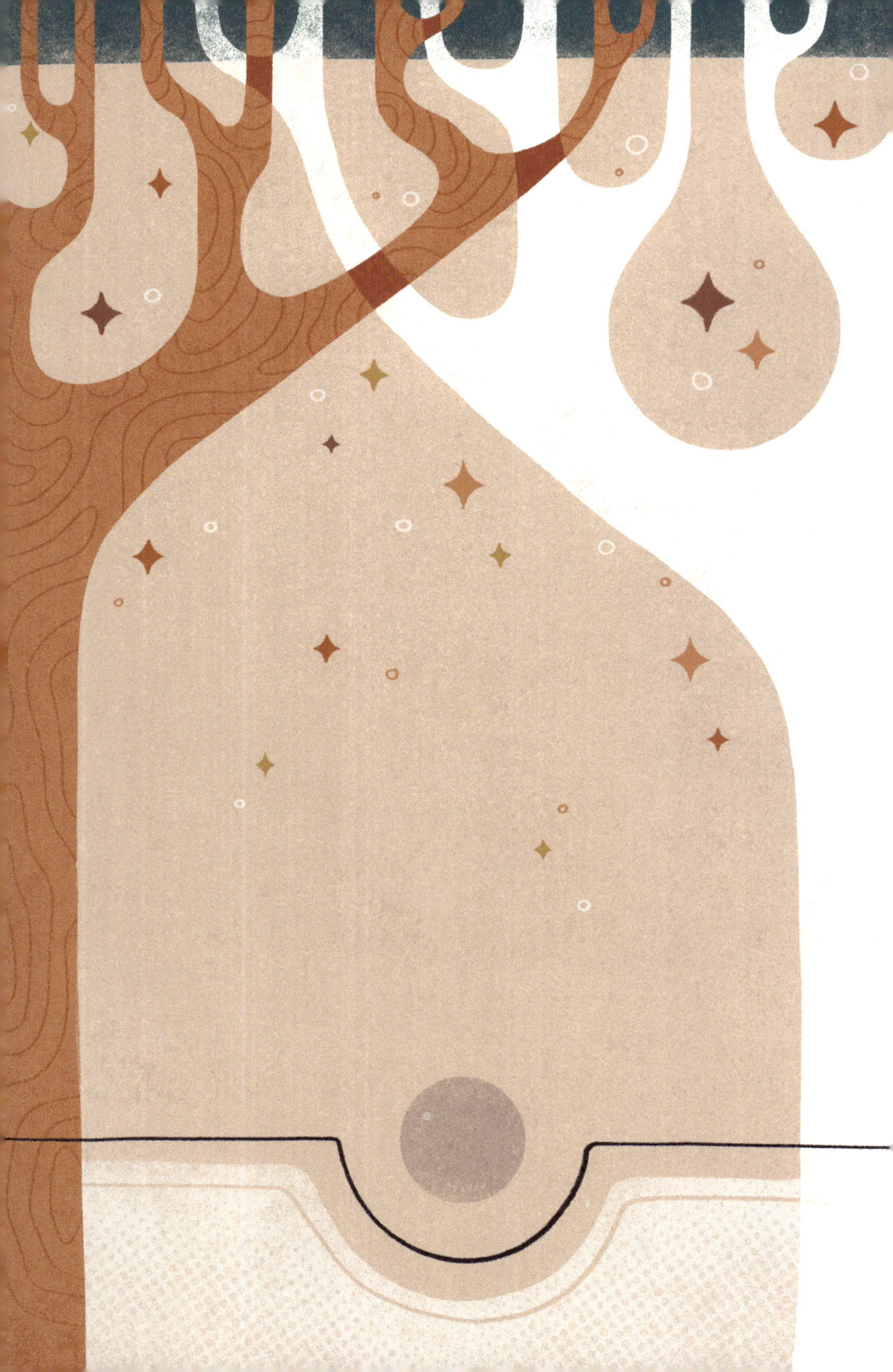

the etymology of you and me

A *shared* meaning,

A *shared* consciousness

That holds space

rather than

FORM.

A timelessness, simultaneously stretching

backwards and forwards ~

weaving together the fabric of our histories

with the creation of our own . . .

- Covella -

An epithet that not only describes the Greek goddess Juno's

Protection & Guidance

During the phase of the New Moon and darkness,

Yet in turn, is innate y representative

then of the counterpart, the WHOLE.

The light,

The bliss,

The vulnerability of having our souls inextricably connected

into

the

i n f i n i t e.

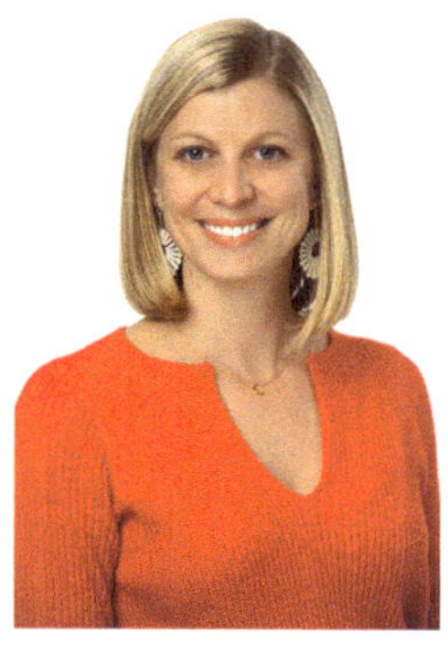

About The Author

Jessica has long been a lover of words and language. Her passion for linguistic expression began in the second grade, when she was presented with the opportunity to take a class studying the foreign language of Spanish. She remembers the teacher saying that if you learned another language, you would be able to connect with new people and different cultures from around the world. Enthralled with this idea, Jessica began her language studies immediately and has continued to follow this passion throughout her life: receiving a Bachelor's degree in Spanish Language and Literature in college from the University of Colorado at Boulder; working with the native Spanish-speaking community in Denver as a bilingual instructional coach; and publishing her first book, *Shine*, and *Brilla* (Spanish edition), in the fall of 2019.

Jessica is also a big advocate for self-expansion and discovery, and along her journey was fortunate to cross paths with her now husband, Thomas. The couple share an affinity for the beauty of the moon and all that it represents, especially the eight unique phases through which it cycles.

jessicacovella.com
jessicacovella@gmail.com

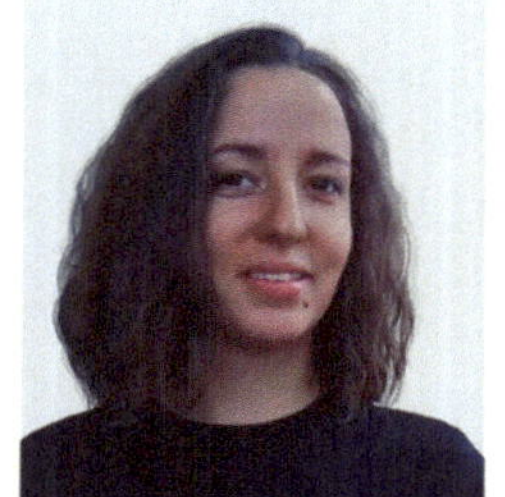

About The Illustrator

Mariia is a young European illustrator. She obtained a Bachelor of Arts Degree in Lviv National Academy of Arts and started the art project "Sestritsy" with her younger sister in 2018. Together they illustrated multiple books and worked on other projects including illustrations for magazines, websites and social media.

sestritsy.com
sestritsy@gmail.com

A Note About My Love of Words

I have always found language utterly fascinating. A way to express that which exists inside, and that which is not yet in existence. The way one can come to understand and use words and language is truly an art form, unique to each individual through which it flows. I hope you enjoy reading the definitions and the origins of some of the words included in this anthology. I invite you to then reread the poem in which a particular word is used, to relish in a deeper experience of why and how I have chosen to play with that particular word in that particular space. Perhaps this exercise will inspire you to incorporate the word or the notion of the word into your own daily expressions, expanding your unique artistry of the elucidation of your human experience as a spiritual being.

1 Frolic

cach·in·nate

/ˈkakəˌnāt/

*verb*RARE

1. laugh loudly.

Origin

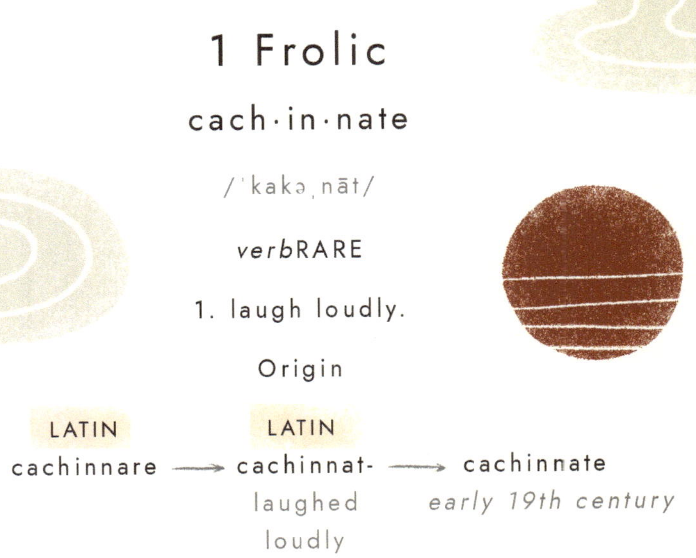

LATIN
cachinnare ⟶ cachinnat- ⟶ cachinnate
laughed   *early 19th century*
loudly

early 19th century: from Latin cachinnat- 'laughed loudly', from the verb cachinnare, of imitative origin ("Cachinnate," 2020).

2 Explosive Expansion

ax·i·om

/ aksēəm/

noun

noun: axiom; plural noun: axioms

1. a statement or proposition which is regarded as being established, accepted, or self-evidently true.

Origin

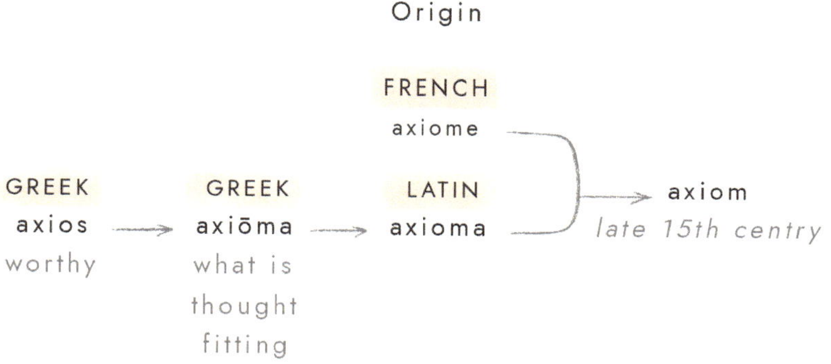

late 15th century: from French axiome or Latin axioma, from Greek axiōma 'what is thought fitting', from axios 'worthy' ("Axiom," 2020).

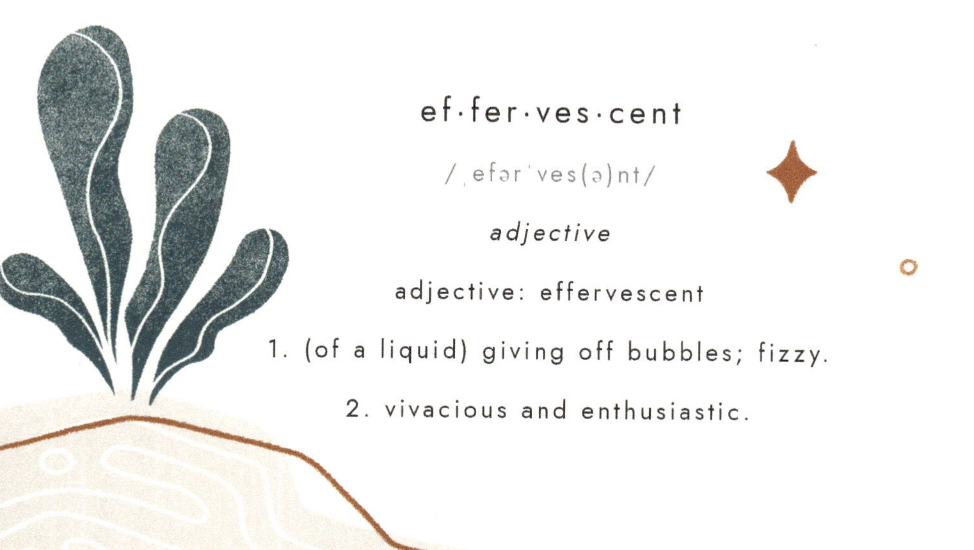

ef·fer·ves·cent

/ˌefərˈves(ə)nt/

adjective

adjective: effervescent

1. (of a liquid) giving off bubbles; fizzy.

2. vivacious and enthusiastic.

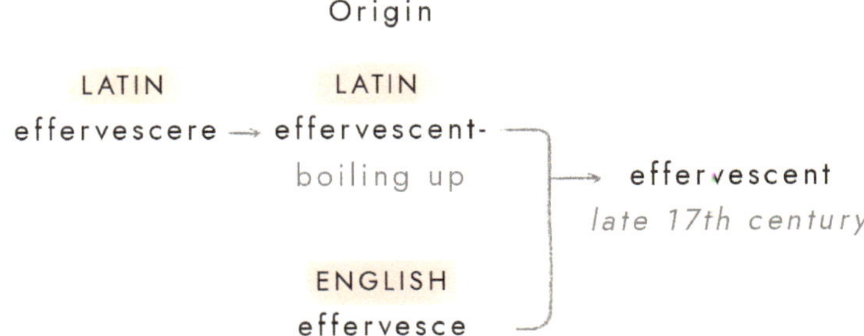

late 17th century: from Latin effervescent- 'boiling up', from the verb effervescere ("Effervescent," 2020).

3 Another World

e·bul·lience

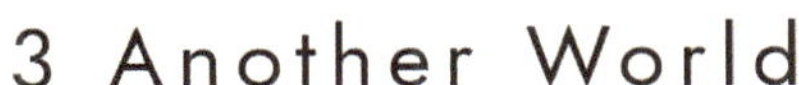

/iˈbo͞olyəns,iˈbəlyəns/

noun

1. the quality of being cheerful and full of energy; exuberance ("Ebullience," 2020).

4 Bricolage

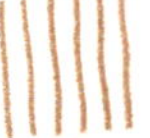

bri·co·lage

/ˌbrēkōˈläZH,ˌbrikə-/

noun

noun: bricolage; plural noun: bricolage; plural noun: bricolages

1. (in art or literature) construction or creation from a diverse range of available things.

2. something constructed or created from a diverse range of available things.

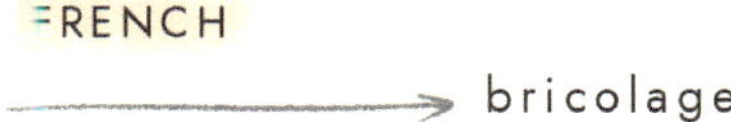

French ("Bricolage", 2020).

¡Mi español!
La expresión de mi entero, por las partes
matizadas de los dos iciomas, de ser
bilingüe

My Spanish!
The expression of my whole self, through the nuanced parts
of both languages, of being
bilingual

5 Vicissitudes of Love

vi·cis·si·tude

/vəˈsisəˌt(y)oōd/

noun

plural noun: vicissitudes

1. a change of circumstances or fortune, typically one that is unwelcome or unpleasant

LITERARY

2. alternation between opposite or contrasting things

Origin

FRENCH

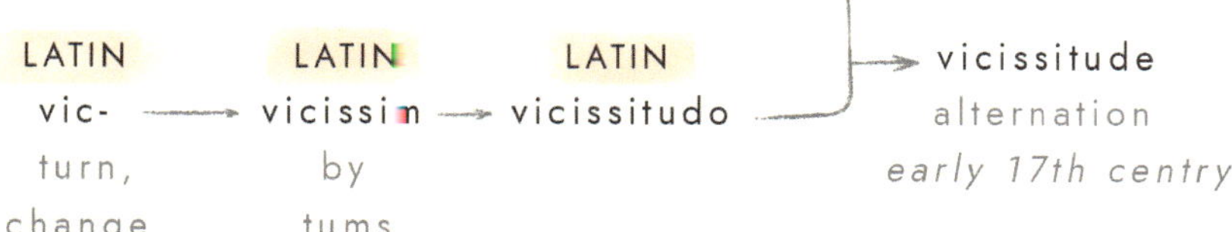

early 17th century (in the sense 'alternation'): from French, or from Latin vicissitudo, from vicissim 'by turns', from vic- 'turn, change' ("Vicissitude," 2020).

ca·coph·o·ny

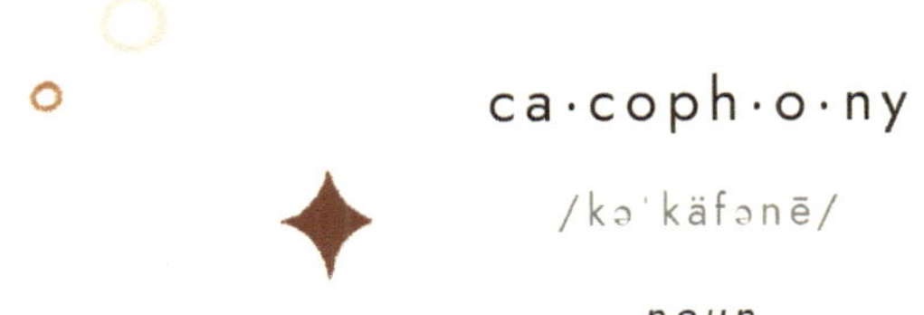

/kəˈkäfənē/

noun

noun: cacophony; plural noun: cacophon es

1. a harsh discordant mixture of sounds

Origin

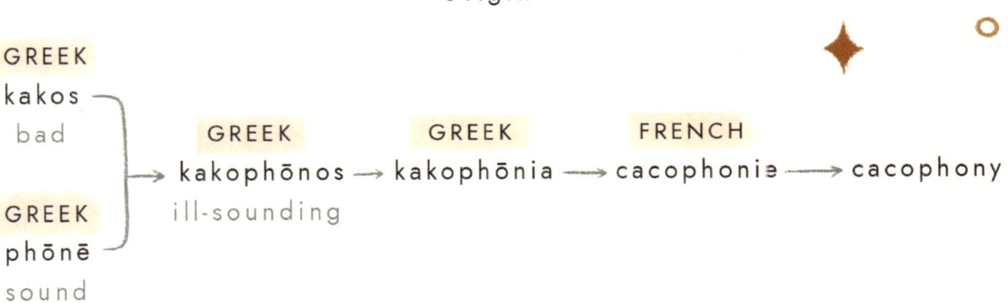

2. mid 17th century: from French cacophonie, from Greek kakophōnia, from kakophōnos 'ill-sounding', from kakos 'bad' + phōnē 'sound' ("Cacophony," 2020).

con·sub·stan·tial

/ˌkänsəbˈstan(t)SH(ə)l/

adjective

adjective: consubstantial

1. of the same substance or essence (used especially of the three persons of the Trinity in Christian theology).

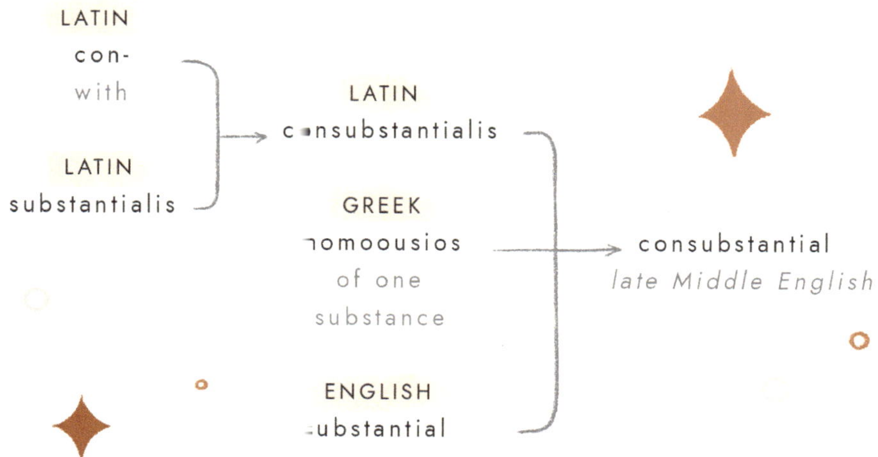

late Middle English: from ecclesiastical Latin consubstantialis (translating Greek homoousios 'of one substance'), from con- 'with' + substantialis ("Consubstantial," 2020).

6 I Can Tell That We Are Going To Be Friends

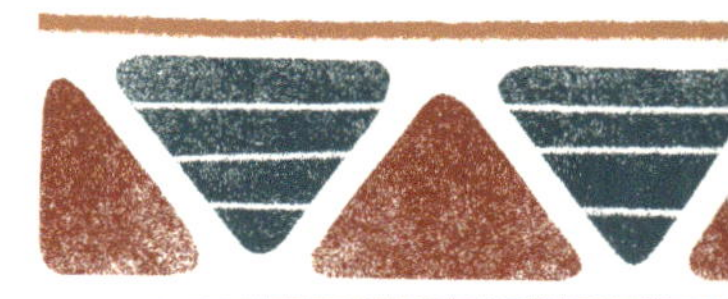

con·so·nance

/ˈkänsənəns/

noun

noun: consonance

1. agreement or compatibility between opinions or actions.
2. the recurrence of similar sounds, especially consonants, in close proximity (chiefly as used in prosody).

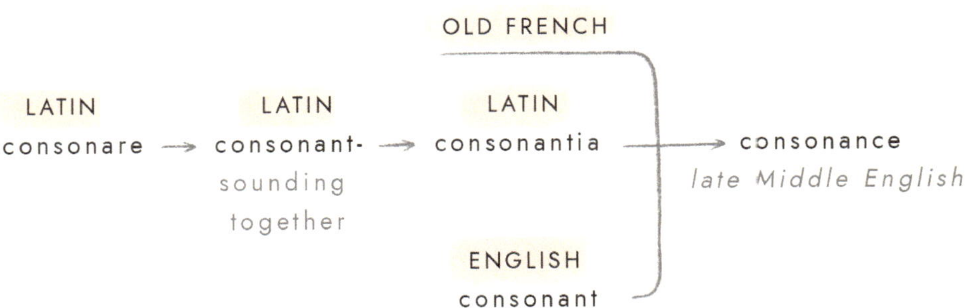

late Middle English: from Old French, or from Latin consonantia, from consonant- 'sounding together', from the verb consonare ("Consonance," 2020)

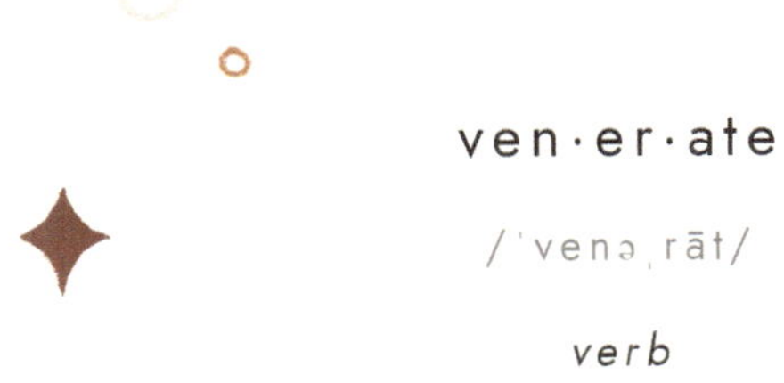

ven·er·ate

/ˈvenəˌrāt/

verb

past tense: venerated; past participle: venerated

1. regard with great respect; revere.

Origin

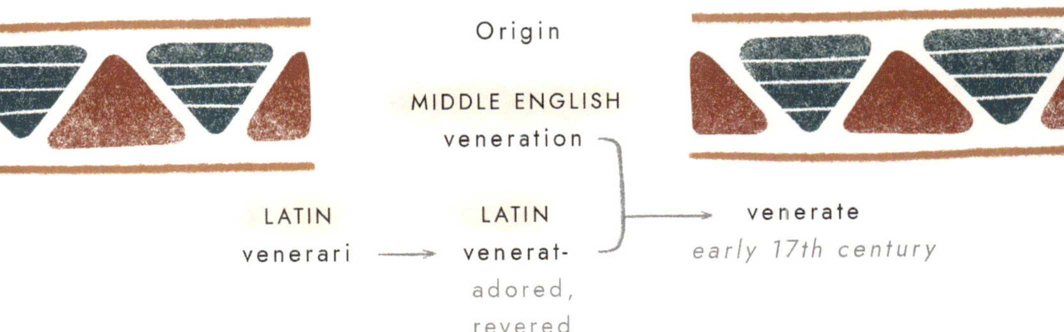

early 17th century (earlier (Middle English) as veneration): from Latin venerat- 'adored, revered', from the verb venerari ("Venerate," 2020)

for·ma·tive

/ˈfôrmədiv/

adjective

1. serving to form something, especially having a profound and lasting influence on a person's development.

2. LINGUISTICS

denoting or relating to any of the smallest meaningful units that are used to form words in a language, typically combining forms and inflections.

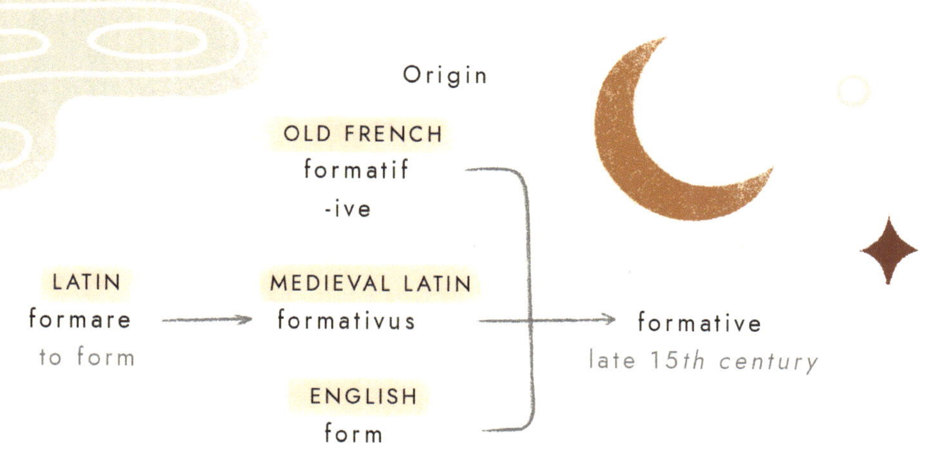

late 15th century: from Old French formatif, -ive or medieval Latin formativus, from Latin formare 'to form' ("Formative," 2020).

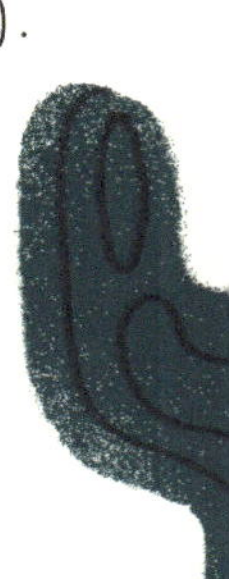

8 The Etymology of You and Me

et·y·mol·o·gy

/ˌedəˈmäləjē/

noun

noun: etymology

1. the study of the origin of words and the way in which their meanings
have changed throughout history.

Origin

late Middle English: from Old French ethimologie, via Latin from Greek
etumologia, from etumologos 'student of etymology', from etumon,
neuter singular of etumos 'true' ("Etymology," 2020).

in·ex·tri·ca·bly

/ˌinəkˈstrikəblē,inˈekstrəkəblē/

adverb

adverb: **inextricably**

1. in a way that is impossible to disentangle or separate
("Inextricably," 2020)

A Note About My Love of Words

e·lu·ci·da·tion

/əˌlo͞osəˈdāSH(ə)n/

noun

noun: **elucidation**; plural noun: **elucidations**

1. explanation that makes something clear; clarification ("Elucidation," 2020).

Works Cited

Etymology. (2020). In Oxford Online Dictionary. Retrieved from
https://en.oxforddictionaries.com/definition/etymology

Cachinnate. (2020). In Oxford Online Dictionary. Retrieved from
https://en.oxforddictionaries.com/definition/cachinnate

Axiom. (2020). In Oxford Online Dictionary. Retrieved from
https://en.oxforddictionaries.com/definition/axiom

Effervescent. (2020). In Oxford Online Dictionary. Retrieved from
https://en.oxforddictionaries.com/definition/effervescent

Ebullience. (2020). In Oxford Online Dictionary. Retrieved from
https://en.oxforddictionaries.com/definition/ebullience

Bricolage. (2020). In Oxford Online Dictionary. Retrieved from
https://en.oxforddictionaries.com/definition/bricolage

Vicissitude. (2020). In Oxford Online Dictionary. Retrieved from
https://en.oxforddictionaries.com/definition/vicissitude

Cacophony. (2020). In Oxford Online Dictionary. Retrieved from
https://en.oxforddictionaries.com/definition/cacophony

Consubstantial. (2020). In Oxford Online Dictionary Retrieved from
https://en.oxforddictionaries.com/definition/consubstantial

Consonance. (2020). In Oxford Online Dictionary. Retrieved from
https://en.oxforddictionaries.com/definition/consonance

Venerate. (2020). In Oxford Online Dictionary. Retrieved from
https://en.oxforddictionaries.com/definition/venerate

Formative. (2020). In Oxford Online Dictionary. Retrieved from
https://en.oxforddictionaries.com/definition/formative

Inextricably. (2020). In Oxford Online Dictionary. Retrieved from
https://en.oxforddictionaries.com/definition/inextricably

Elucidation. (2020). In Oxford Online Dictionary. Retrieved from
https://en.oxforddictionaries.com/definition/elucidation

9 781733 331159